# Why You Really Can Memorize Scripture

Understand and unlock your mind's
natural ability to memorize long passages

# Why You Really Can Memorize Scripture

Understand and unlock your mind's
natural ability to memorize long passages

Dr. Daniel Morris

LIFE SENTENCE
—Publishing, LLC—

*Why You Really Can Memorize Scripture*
Dr. Daniel Morris – Copyright © 2012

All Bible verses taken from the King James Version

PRINTED IN THE UNITED STATES OF AMERICA

First edition published 2012

LIFE SENTENCE Publishing books are available at discounted prices for ministries and other outreach. Find out more by contacting info@lifesentencepubishing.com

LIFE SENTENCE Publishing
and its logo are trademarks of

LIFE SENTENCE Publishing, LLC
P.O. BOX 652
Abbotsford, WI 54405

www.lifesentencepublishing.com

Like us on Facebook

ISBN: 978-1-62245-039-8

# Dedication

*This book is dedicated to the members of our church who enrolled in the three-year ministry of discipleship – and have never given up. Since memorization of long passages of Scripture is a part of their spiritual training, I wrote this book primarily to help them accomplish that goal. The example of their dedication is a most effective motivation for others not only to begin discipleship – but to finish it. They have been a great encouragement to me, for which I am very grateful. The book also is dedicated to my wife, Debbie, who for so many years has glorified God through a humble, unassuming faithfulness to His calling.*

# Contents

# Introduction

As a teenager called to be a missionary, I had a great desire to fulfill God's will, but I also had a great sense of inadequacy for such an extraordinary purpose. A great source of encouragement to me was God's promise that he who meditates in His Word "shall be like a tree planted by the rivers of water, that bringeth forth his fruit in his season; his leaf also shall not wither; and whatsoever he doeth shall prosper" (Psalm 1:3).

Now that was something I could do! It gave me real hope that God would make my missionary service prosper, if by faith in His promise, I did my part to meditate on His Word.

Part of meditation is to memorize God's Word, so I began a systematic habit of memorizing consecutive passages of Scripture. Through the years I learned, both by study and by experience, how God made our memory function. This helped greatly in this blessed task. Presently, I have 42 chapters memorized and, best of all, our missionary work has prospered beyond what I could have imagined.

— ⟨ღ⟩ —

# Your Memory Is God's Creation – And It Works!

The memory is a fantastic function of the incredible brain that God created in man. All of the technology on earth has not produced anything close to its efficiency and capability. You wake up in the morning and your memory is already functioning. Even though you do not consciously realize it, you remember how to get up, and you remember how the pillow, the blanket, and the nightstand feel. You remember where the door is and where the bathroom is. You remember where the bathroom articles are and how the sink and the shower work.

Everything you do during the day depends on your memory. Your brain automatically processes information in three steps: codifying, archiving, and recovering information. Without memory you would live as a mental vegetable, because intelligence depends on the memory to produce activity, reason, communication, planning, and achievement.

After a while, however, you may notice that you forgot to turn on the coffee maker like you had planned. You worry about your bad memory in spite of the fact that everything you have done has depended upon its proper function. Because of this, you might ask, *Why does my memory work for some things and not for some other things?* That is the wise question that you need to consider, and the purpose of this book will be to answer that question and to teach you how to make use of your memory to its fullest capacity in memorizing Scripture.

First, you need to understand that when we say *the memory*, in reality we are speaking of several different functions of the brain. A computer has temporary memory and permanent memory. When someone is writing a letter on a computer, the work is being saved temporarily in the microchips or in a temporary section of the hard drive. In order for the work to be saved in permanent memory, it has to be saved to the permanent area of the hard drive. If you have not saved your work, and all of a sudden there is a power failure, you will lose all of the unsaved work.

The human memory is much more complicated, but, in a way similar to that of a computer. Your memory actually consists of different types of memory. The simplest type of memory is called *environmental memory*, which is the instantaneous ability to recognize the environment by way of the five senses. When you get up in the morning, as I mentioned, and touch the nightstand with your hand – even without seeing it – you know what you are touching. The permanent area of the memory recognizes the feel and hardness of the wood, and the form and shape of the nightstand. However, the act itself – or, in other words, the experience in that instant of touching the nightstand – will be forgotten within a few seconds after touching it. In the course of a day, the five senses work in conjunction with the memory to recognize thousands of things, but this memory is not saved unless something catches your attention or is considered important in some way.

The act of giving some level of attention or importance to some experience will result in the second type of memory, which is commonly called *short-term memory.* This type of memory is said to be contained in the prefrontal cortex of the brain. If I turn on the coffee maker and there is a certain interest or importance in drinking a cup of coffee, the short-term memory will probably remind me to go back in a few minutes to get my cup of coffee. If there is not enough attention paid or importance given, or if my attention is distracted by other matters, it is possible that I will forget to go back to the coffee maker. This type of memory is short and dependent on attention and importance. Even if I remember to drink my coffee, in a few hours or days – if I don't think about it for some reason – that incident will be lost from my memory and I will not remember having done it.

However, if you were drinking your coffee on September 11 2001, and turned on the television in time to see the terrorists crash their planes into the World Trade Center in New York City, and experienced the horror of watching thousands of people perish when the twin towers fell, it is quite probable that even today, years later, not only do you remember seeing that terrible event, you also remember where you were and that you were drinking your coffee. The impact was such that not only was the event engraved in your permanent memory, but so also were many insignificant things related to that experience. You have experienced the third type of memory, which is called *long-term memory*.

This type of memory is apparently located in the area of the brain called the hippocampus and can be divided into at least three classes. The first class is *process memory* and is the most permanent of all. Some things, once learned, are never forgotten, even if they are not repeated for years. Examples of this include riding a bicycle, driving a car, tying a knot, or swimming.

The second class of long-term memory is called *declarative memory*. This class saves informational data. Data is received quickly and lost quickly if it only stimulates the short-term memory. However, if the data is considered important and there is some degree of interest in it, or, in some cases, if it is very strange, it will be engraved in this class of long-term memory. This is the class of memory in which we are most interested because it is here that we will permanently memorize Scripture.

The third class is called *foundational memory,* which saves experiences from early ages. Some of these memories may be considered important, while others may not seem to have the least bit of significance. Because of this, foundational memory is the most mysterious of the three. However, a significant detail for our consideration is the way in which some memories are not forgotten because they are associated with another memory. Utilizing association of memories is very useful in effective Scripture memorization.

# CHAPTER TWO

# How Understanding Your Memory Will Help and Encourage You to Memorize

In a simplified way I have illustrated three different levels, or sections, of the memory. In reality, the memory is not that simple. Each individual section actually has many different levels or classes. However, what is actually important for now is to understand that for something to be stored in the memory, there is a process that occurs at different levels until it reaches a more permanent section.

At this point you might ask, "What does this have to do with memorizing Scripture?" The answer is that the obstacles that most hinder the memorization of Scripture are frustration and discouragement that result from attempting to memorize verses, and in a short time, no longer being able to remember what you memorized. This experience – together with other experiences of forgetting names, occasions, dates, and other similar things – can produce an attitude of concluding that your memory does not function adequately enough to memorize Scripture. Nothing hinders the process of memorizing more than accepting the conclusion that "I can't memorize."

This conclusion is all too common in many people, and even though it seems to be based on the experience of a poor memory, in reality it is based on the lack of understanding about how memory functions. When one understands the marvelous capability of the brain that God created, and how in reality it is functioning continuously and correctly each moment, one realizes that the conclusion "I can't memorize" is mistaken, and, on the contrary, it gives one a new hope that there truly is a way one can memorize. The old saying, "If you say you can or if you say you can't, you're right," explains the primary reason why some can memorize and others can't memorize.

When one understands how the memory functions at different levels and even in different parts of the brain, one discovers that the problem is simply not achieving the storage of Scripture in long-term memory, because the necessary steps to stimulate that section of the memory were lacking. In this booklet, I will attempt to explain these steps in a clear and practical way so that you can experience the ability to memorize portions of the Word of God.

# CHAPTER THREE

# Key Commands of God Depend on Long-Term Memory of Scripture

Even though you are convinced that it is possible to memorize Scripture, you still might not do it because you are not convinced it is necessary. This is the second greatest hindrance and has to do with one's faith, hope, and values.

Different people will have different reasons for feeling the need to memorize verses of the Bible. Some people simply like memorizing and they're not very concerned about the work involved. For others, however, the amount of work involved in memorizing is the main reason for their decision to do so or not. Some feel the need to honor God by memorizing Scripture, while others are satisfied with other ways of serving God.

In the end, what will most determine the decision to memorize Scripture or not are the questions: Do the benefits outweigh the work? Is it really worth it to memorize? Now, besides the matter of whether those questions show spiritual maturity or not, God's answer is a firm "yes."

One of God's most serious and emphatic admonitions is found in Deuteronomy 6:4–12, where He says, "Hear, O Israel: The LORD our God is one LORD: And thou shalt love the LORD thy God with all thine heart, and with all thy soul, and with all thy might. And these words, which I command thee this day, shall be in thine heart: And thou shalt teach them diligently unto thy children, and shalt talk of them when thou sittest in thine house, and when thou walkest by the way, and when thou liest down, and when thou risest up. And thou shalt bind them for a sign upon thine hand, and they shall be as frontlets between thine eyes. And thou shalt write them upon the posts of thy house, and on thy gates. And it shall be, when the LORD thy God shall have brought thee into the land which he sware unto thy fathers, to Abraham, to Isaac, and to Jacob, to give thee great and goodly cities, which thou buildedst not, And houses full of all good things, which thou filledst not, and wells digged, which thou diggedst not, vineyards and olive trees, which thou plantedst not; when thou shalt have eaten and be full; Then beware lest thou forget the LORD, which brought thee forth out of the land of Egypt, from the house of bondage."

Obviously, one needs to have Scripture verses memorized in order to "talk of them when thou sittest in thine house, and when thou walkest by the way, and when thou liest down, and when thou risest up." Only by knowing passages of the Word of God by memory will one be able to fulfill this commandment that is so important in life. For Israel, only through the Word of God would the next generation know God himself. Sadly, this fervent admonition was not followed. In Judges 2:10, God says, "And also all that generation were gathered unto their fathers: and there arose another generation after them, which knew not the LORD, nor yet the works which he had done for Israel." This ignorance of the Word of God and, as a result, not knowing God himself, left the next generation so spiritually weak that they strayed into the sinful paths of the world and suffered terrible consequences. One must not take lightly the need to know by memory and continually repeat the Word of God.

On the other hand, God offers promises and prosperity to those who have His words in their mind and heart and meditate upon them. God told Joshua, "This book of the law shall not depart out of thy mouth; but thou shalt meditate therein day and night, that thou mayest observe to do according to all that is written therein: for then thou shalt make thy way prosperous, and then thou shalt have good success" (Joshua 1:8).

Psalm 1 expresses the same promise, saying, "Blessed is the man that walketh not in the counsel of the ungodly, nor standeth in the way of sinners, nor sitteth in the seat of the scornful. But his delight is in the law of the LORD; and in his law doth he meditate day and night. And he shall be like a tree planted by the rivers of water, that bringeth forth his fruit in his season; his leaf also shall not wither; and whatsoever he doeth shall prosper. The ungodly are not so: but are like the chaff which the wind driveth away. Therefore the ungodly shall not stand in the judgment, nor sinners in the congregation of the righteous. For the LORD knoweth the way of the righteous: but the way of the ungodly shall perish."

David also spoke of the security that God promises to those who guard His Word in their hearts. He said, "The righteous shall inherit the land, and dwell therein for ever. The mouth of the righteous speaketh wisdom, and his tongue talketh of judgment. The law of his God is in his heart; none of his steps shall slide" (Psalm 37:29–31).

Besides this, the memorized Word of God is also a protection against the traps of sin as we read in Psalm 119:11, "Thy word have I hid in mine heart, that I might not sin against thee."

As we are to walk in the steps of Jesus, perhaps His example is the most important. When the devil tempted Him in the desert, He always responded by repeating from memory the Word of God like a weapon against the deceit of the enemy. Matthew 4:3–4 describes the first incident. "And when the tempter came to him, he said, If thou be the Son of God, command that these stones be made bread. But he answered and said, It is written, Man shall not live by bread alone, but by every word that proceedeth out of the mouth of God."

Not only the devil, but also the Pharisees, Sadducees, priests, and scribes attempted to trap our Lord in some error. Time after time our Master's response was the Word of God repeated from memory.

The apostle Peter admonished Christians to "sanctify the Lord God in your hearts: and be ready always to give an answer to every man that asketh you a reason of the hope that is in you with meekness and fear" (1 Peter 3:15). There is no better preparation "to be ready always to give an answer" than to be able to repeat from memory the Word of God. Paul called the Word of God our "sword of the Spirit" to battle against and defeat the devil. To have Scripture memorized is to be armed and protected every moment. To not have Scripture memorized is to be exposed on many occasions to spiritual warfare – unarmed.

Christian maturity is described in Romans 12:2 as a process of ceasing to be "conformed to this world" and being "transformed by the renewing of your mind [in other words, of your thinking], that ye may prove what is that good, and acceptable, and perfect, will of God." Therefore, a change in our thinking is indispensable for Christian victory. What better way to transform our thinking than to have the very thoughts of God kept in the memory of our mind?

The command of Colossians 3:16 is to "Let the word of Christ dwell in you *richly* [emphasis added] [plousios: copiously, abundantly, richly] in all wisdom; teaching and admonishing one another in psalms and hymns and spiritual songs, singing with grace in your hearts to the Lord." This does not give us a picture of little memorization, but of abundant memorization. Still more, our Lord commanded us to be the light of the world and the salt of the earth. He told us, very directly, that hidden light is worthless and salt without flavor is as useless as trash that is thrown out. This light and salt represent a Christian's influence that illuminates and preserves so that others might be saved from condemnation and darkness. This influence consists of a testimony of life that reflects the life of Christ and the Word of God that is spoken and proclaimed to others. In order to be light and salt in this world, we must be ready to evangelize and teach others spontaneously. Again, this will depend on the amount of Scripture that we have memorized and have available to use to illuminate the lives of others in the matter of salvation and the way of Christ.

We must recognize, humbly, that our God-given memory was not to be used only for the temporal things of this world. It is a function created by God for great purposes described in His Word. Its use for these purposes will bring abundance of power and well-being to our lives, our families, and our ministries. To fail to use our memory for the purposes of God will bring consequences that will be a detriment to our lives, our families, and our ministries – more than we normally comprehend.

To summarize, the greatest hindrances to memorization of Scripture are: an attitude of thinking that "I can't memorize," and an attitude of doubting that the benefits of memorizing Scripture outweigh the work involved. The first hindrance is overcome when one understands how the memory functions, and the second is eliminated when one considers what God Himself says about the benefits of memorizing His Word and the consequences of not doing so.

# CHAPTER FOUR

# An Overview of The Steps to Memorizing Scripture

Now I would like to mention the most important principle involved in memorizing verses of the Bible. The secret is this: Establish a certain amount of *time daily* to memorize and not a certain number of verses. Do not worry about the number of verses that you memorize. Just determine to give your best effort during a certain amount of time each day.

I would suggest that you begin with ten minutes a day. Any person is able to simply apply the techniques that will be presented in this article for ten minutes without the stress of having to achieve a certain number of verses in that time. This eliminates the pressure to advance and the discouragement that can result from that pressure. Only think of giving God your very best for ten minutes and be satisfied when you have completed the time. Of course, sometimes it is enjoyable to memorize a passage and you will go beyond the ten minutes. However, there is no pressure when you do it because you want to, instead of because you have to. If, the next day, you cannot remember anything, do not worry. Apply the techniques again to the best of your ability on the same verse for another ten minutes. If, on the third day you still cannot remember the verse, even so, do not worry. Simply fulfill this short daily period of time once again.

You might think that you will be memorizing the same verse forever, but I assure you that this will not be the case. When you simply give your best effort for an established time and let what God has created work to achieve the goal of memorizing His Word, you will be surprised at how much you will be able to memorize during one month, and astonished at what you will be able to memorize in one year. Success in memorization does not depend on capability, but rather on consistency. God took charge of the matter of capability. Just appreciate what He has done and decide to discipline yourself to use it as He designed, for a certain amount of time daily.

Have you prepared your heart with the understanding of the need to memorize Scripture, and do you trust the capability of the memory to function as God has designed? If so, we will now study four initial, practical steps that will give your memory what it needs to assimilate, store, and later recall verses of Scripture.

The first step is to read the verse several times just to know what it says. However, the memory functions much better with what you understand and, on the other hand, it struggles with what you do not understand. Because of this, the second step is to achieve a better understanding by answering some questions about the verse, such as follows:

- Who wrote it?

- Was it one of the prophets or an apostle?

- Who was this person?

- To whom was the verse written?

- Was it written to a particular person, city, church, or to some group of people?

- Under what circumstances was it written?

- What was happening in the life of the person, town, church, or people?

- Why was it written?

- What purpose did God have to speak this message, through the writer, in that time?

- What is the message for us today?

Answering and meditating on these questions will not only help you know the words of the verse, but also help you clearly understand what you're reading. In addition, you will begin to achieve the spiritual benefits of memorizing Scripture that were mentioned previously.

After getting to know and understand the verse, the third step is to analyze the structure of the verse. Notice if it is a complete sentence, if it is more than one complete sentence, or if it is a part of a sentence. Look for periods, commas, and other punctuation marks. How is the verse divided by these punctuation marks, and how many divisions does it have? How many phrases are there, and what are they? How many thoughts are in the verse, separated by punctuation? Also, observe the words of the verse. Notice the nouns, verbs, and adjectives. Does it mention people, places, or events? Are there commands? Is there any other significant form of grammar?

Another part of analyzing the structure is to concentrate on the first word of the verse and its relation to the previous verse. Does it complete a sentence or answer a question? Does it explain or continue the previous verse? The first word is like a door to the rest of the verse for your memory. If you remember the first word, the door will be open to the rest of the verse. If not, it will be a closed door to the rest. Normally, understanding its relation to the previous verse is very helpful to remembering the first word of a verse.

The first three steps should actually only take three to five minutes, depending on how long or complex the verse is. The fourth step is the least known, yet the most efficient in helping your memory store the verse in its long-term section. This step consists in finding *curiosities* in the verse that can catch the attention of your memory. I call these curiosities *nails* because they are details that rapidly stick in long-term memory and also stimulate the memory to remember other information in the verse that is associated with them. In other words, they *nail* the phrases of the verse to your long-term memory.

Things that are odd, unusual, or strange stimulate the memory much more than things that are normal and common. Also, order or patterns stimulate the memory more than something that is without order. Because of this, it is of enormous help to find, or even to invent, *nails* in the verse in order to memorize it more easily, rapidly, and permanently.

You may find similarities between two or more words. They might have the same prefixes or suffixes or, even better, they may rhyme. In other cases you may find alliterations, or several words that start with the same letter. Some verses have words whose first letters form a word. These acrostics are especially useful to the memory.

Other verses have similarities related to the number of words. It might be that the phrases have the same number of words, or perhaps the number of words increases or decreases in sequence (three, four, and five words; or five, four, and three). Another possibility is to find a pattern of numbers of words, or of symmetry in the number (four, three, four, three; or four, five, four). Once again, these curiosities will stick more easily in your memory and make it easier to remember the related words.

Similarities in the order of the words are another possibility. In some cases there are keywords whose first letters are in alphabetical order. In other cases there may be a chronological order to the words or to the principal ideas of the verse. You will be surprised at how many different types of *nails* or curiosities exist and how much they help your memory.

Sometimes we can easily find these *nails* in the nature or structure of the verse, as in the case of similarities in words, numbers, and order. Sometimes, however, if there does not appear to be any we can invent them. One example of inventing nails is to take the first letter of the key words and make a strange sentence with words using the same first letters. The strange sentence will easily stick in your memory, giving you the first letters of the key words of the verse. This will help you recall the entire verse.

I have heard Dr. John Goetsch, a world renowned evangelist, explain how the rhythm of walking as you memorize helps you memorize more quickly and efficiently. It would be wise to try this also.

Don't worry if this brief description seems complicated or confusing. In the next chapter I will go through each step with an example; and you will see how truly usable these steps are.

# CHAPTER FIVE

# Applying The Steps

In this chapter you will see an example of how to apply the previously mentioned practical steps toward memorizing Scripture. Before proceeding, however, I would like to mention two different types of Scripture memorization. The first, and most common, is the memorization of selected verses that deal with and fulfill specific needs. The first selected verse I memorized as a child was John 3:16. Later, I memorized the verses of "The Romans Road." In Vacation Bible Schools and Bible College it is common to have to memorize selected verses.

The second type of memorization involves long, consecutive passages of Scripture. At one point in my life, I decided to memorize an entire epistle, little by little. It was a way for me to meditate day and night on the Scripture, and it was also a very worthy challenge. Eventually, I memorized the book of Philippians and was amazed at how much more I understood the heart and teachings of this epistle after committing it to memory, rather than when I had just read and studied it. This has been my main purpose of memorization ever since.

Both types of memorization are worthy, necessary, and valuable. However, there is one major difference between the two types. If you memorize selected verses, it is essential to memorize the *address* or location of the verse. On the other hand, when memorizing large portions of Scripture, it is not practical or even helpful to memorize the location except for the first and last verses, or the number of the entire chapter.

Now, let's look at Colossians 1:16. "For by him were all things created, that are in heaven, and that are in earth, visible and invisible, whether they be thrones, or dominions, or principalities, or powers: all things were created by him, and for him."

I chose this verse randomly, trying to avoid the most common verses in order to have a fresh memorization experience.

First, carefully read the verse four times.

Second, meditate on the message.

- Who wrote these words and to whom?

- Why did he write this to them?

- What message does God have for us in this verse?

He speaks of Christ as the creator of all, both above and below. Nothing in creation exists, either physical or spiritual, without Him. No power or authority exists that is not under Him, and all exist to serve His purpose. The more you learn about this verse, the more it will strengthen and profit you.

Third, look at the structure of the verse.

- There are eight commas.

- More importantly, did you notice the two main parts separated by a colon?

- The first part is much longer, so how can we *divide and conquer* it?

- Notice that there is a declaration: "*For by him were all things created.*"

- Following the declaration is a list of four
  pairs of things He created.

In the following graph, I have organized this verse as we would look at it in our mind. It may take a few minutes to analyze this diagram, but once you understand how to see the structure of any verse, it will only take a few seconds to do so.

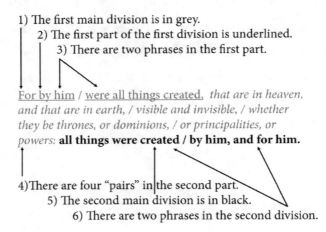

1) The first main division is in grey.
  2) The first part of the first division is underlined.
    3) There are two phrases in the first part.

For by him / were all things created, *that are in heaven, and that are in earth, / visible and invisible, / whether they be thrones, or dominions, / or principalities, or powers:* **all things were created / by him, and for him.**

4) There are four "pairs" in the second part.
  5) The second main division is in black.
    6) There are two phrases in the second division.

Let's reorganize the divisions and parts to illustrate more clearly how to look at the structure of this verse. You do not actually have to re-write a verse, although it would be very helpful if you wanted to.

<u>For by him</u> / <u>were all things created,</u>
> *Two phrases*

that are in heaven, and that are in earth,
> *First "pair" - heaven and earth*

visible and invisible,
> *Second "pair" - visible and invisible*

whether they be thrones, or dominions,
> *Third "pair" - thrones or dominions*

or principalities, or powers:
> *Fourth "pair" - principalities or powers*

**all things were created / by him, and for him.**
> *Two phrases*

Fourth, what are the curiosities or *nails* in this verse? The structure provides a useful pattern: two phrases - four pairs - two phrases.

Within the four pairs, the first two fit together: *"that are in heaven and that are in earth, visible and invisible"*

The last two also fit together: *"whether they be thrones or dominions or principalities or powers"*

Notice also how the words *"that are in"* are repeated in the first set of pairs.

Do you see how the word "*or*" is repeated between each word of the last two sets of pairs?

Also, notice the similarity of the beginning "*For by him*" and the end "*for him.*"

Since the bulk of the verse consists of the four pairs, we could even invent a *nail* by forming an odd sentence using the first letters of each word in the four pairs: heaven, earth, visible, invisible, thrones, dominions, principalities, powers (h, e, v, i, t, d, p, p)

Would this stick in your mind?

*Happy elephants vacuum in their dark purple pants.*

Try making your own, and remember, the stranger the better.

— ❧ —

# CHAPTER SIX

# Applying The Steps (Part II)

Now, let's actually memorize Colossians 1:16. "For by him were all things created, that are in heaven, and that are in earth, visible and invisible, whether they be thrones, or dominions, or principalities, or powers: all things were created by him, and for him." Look at the way we organized the verse according to its different parts in the last chapter, and memorize the first phrase, "For by him." Think of Christ, think that there are three words, and repeat them without looking. This will stick quickly in short-term memory, so understand that but do not be satisfied. Long-term memory is the goal.

After repeating the first phrase by memory about five more times, think of Christ's work of creation and memorize the second phrase, "were all things created." There are four words in this phrase, so notice that there are three words in the first phrase and four in the second: 3 - 4. Repeat this phrase again until it sticks in your memory.

Go back and repeat the first phrase again. It may be easy or it may not be. If you are already forgetting it, don't worry. That is how short-term memory works, and by repeating it again, you will work it into a longer-term area. Now, repeat the second phrase again (remember 3 - 4). Next, repeat them both together until you can say them by memory fairly easily.

Next, we will work on the first of the four pairs: "that are in heaven and that are in earth." Think of heaven as being more important than earth so you remember that it is first. You can also remember *happy elephants* from the odd sentence to give you the first letters. Notice the words "that are in" are repeated for heaven and for earth. With this in mind, repeat "that are in heaven and that are in earth" many times until it seems you are exaggerating.

Again, repeat the first phrase, "For by him," and then the second, "were all things created." Repeat them together, "For by him were all things created," and afterwards repeat the first pair, "that are in heaven and that are in earth." Finally, repeat them all together until you can say them comfortably. "For by him were all things created, that are in heaven, and that are in earth." For the sake of time, let's call this the *repeat-and-add sequence.*

Now, work on the second pair. Use the odd sentence, *happy elephants vacuum in,* to remember the first letters of the key words "visible – invisible." Also, notice that they are going backwards in relation to the first pair (*visible* relates to earth first, and *invisible* relates to heaven). If details like this help your memory, use them. If not, look for something else. Repeat this second pair, "visible and invisible" many times, and then do the repeat-and-add sequence with what you have already memorized.

Next, work on the third pair, "whether they be thrones, or dominions." Do you notice that there are actually two sets of two pairs (two *quads*)? In each quad the first pair is longer and the second is shorter. Also, compare the words "that are in" from the first pair with the words "whether they be" from the third pair. Visualize Christ's authority over all things in addition to His power of creation. Remember the words from the odd sentence, *happy elephants vacuum in their dark,* to remember the first letters of the key words. Repeat this phrase many times and do the repeat-and-add sequence.

Now go on to the fourth pair, "or principalities, or powers." Notice how each of the key words of the last two pairs is connected with *or.* Also, these last two key words begin with the same letter *p.* Again, use the odd sentence (*purple pants*) to remember these two letters. Repeat the phrase several times and then use the repeat-and-add sequence.

Finally, work on the second division of the verse, "all things were created by him, and for him." Notice that the words of the first phrase of the second division, "were all things," are the same words as the second phrase of the first division, "all things were," except that the place of "were" is changed. (This is another interesting detail that can help the memory.) Use the repeat-and-add sequence and go to the last phrase. Notice the similarity of the last phrase and the first phrase. After using the repeat-and-add sequence one more time, you now have successfully stored the complete verse in short-term memory.

If you are memorizing this as a selected verse, repeat the address, Colossians 1:16, every time you say the verse. If you are memorizing it as part of the entire chapter, this is not necessary. In both cases, the next task is to store the verse in long-term memory. The first step to do this is to wait for a short time and then repeat the verse again. Within an hour there may be a struggle to remember it, or you may not remember it at all. Do not let this discourage you. It is part of the natural process of the memory as we have discussed before. If you have time to review it again, do so by using the repeat-and-add sequence, to restore it into your memory. If not, wait and do so during your ten-minute period the next day. When the struggle to remember the verse after a period of time diminishes, it is because the verse is passing to areas of long-term memory in the brain.

Remember to meditate on the meaning and purpose of the verse, because this not only helps the memory, but it is one of the most important reasons to memorize. Also, remember the curiosities or *nails*, because these will stick the verse in long-term memory rapidly. After it is well memorized, you may find that you no longer need the *nails*, but it is perfectly acceptable if you continue to use them.

# CHAPTER SEVEN

# How to Keep Your Verses and Not Lose Them

Memorizing Scripture is not like memorizing answers for a test and not caring if you remember afterwards. We want to keep our verses memorized forever – to honor God and to receive the blessings of His Word permanently.

At this point we have to face the cold fact that if we do not repeat what we have memorized, we will lose it. I have heard it said that if you repeat something a certain number of times, you will not forget it. That simply does not work. True, some verses like John 3:16, "The Romans Road," or Psalm 23 may stick in your permanent memory and not need repeating. That is not the normal case, however. The problem is, as I memorize more and more Scripture verses, when am I going to find the time to repeat them all?

Fortunately, there is a solution to the problem. If you form a simple, daily habit, you will not have to take any extra time from your schedule to keep your verses memorized. How can this be? The secret is to use some daily routine that is done instinctively without need of concentration.

For me, the routine of showering, shaving, brushing teeth, and dressing is more than enough time to repeat two chapters of Scripture daily. Try reading a chapter as slowly as you might repeat it by memory, and you will be surprised that it only takes three or four minutes. How long does it take you to get ready each day?

Whether it is your getting-ready time, your running or commuting time, or some other daily routine, the problem is not in finding the time; it is in forming the habit.

At first, your mind will experience distractions, and it does take some willful concentration to get accustomed to saying your verses during whatever routine you choose. However, it is not only an achievable way to completely solve the time problem, but it is also a spiritually strengthening habit that turns your memorized verses into daily blessings.

Here is the plan that I have used to remember entire chapters:

- Memorize a verse in your ten-minute daily time until it is well memorized.

- Transfer the memorized verse to your routine time and repeat it daily.

- Continue adding memorized verses to your routine time until two chapters are complete.

- After two chapters are memorized, repeat your new verses daily along with only one previously memorized chapter. Alternate the previously memorized chapters daily.

- When a new chapter is complete, keep repeating it daily along with one of the previous chapters for a week or two. Then add it to your alternating chapters. (You might postpone memorizing new verses while you do this, but be very careful not to allow this to break your habit of memorizing).

A similar plan can be formed to remember groups of selected verses.

Your ability to repeat memorized verses will vary from day to day. Some days it will be a breeze and you will finish in no time at all. Other days it will not be so easy and it may seem like some verses or phrases have been lost.

It is of the utmost importance, again, not to let this be a matter of pressure that can cause discouragement. This variation is normal. Expect it. Sometimes what seems to be forgotten one day will come clearly to mind on another day. In many cases you can simply skip over a part that does not come to your mind, and continue with what does come, knowing that it is all still there and will show up next time.

In other cases, you will need to read and reinforce a verse or phrase that did not stick in your long-term memory. This also is normal. Some things just need to be reinforced. Many times these reinforced parts will become the most completely memorized of all. Make it a matter of meditation, devotions, and a greater under-standing of God's Word as you reinforce these parts. In any case, simply continue your plan of ten minutes or more a day of memorization and of repeating the memorized verses during your routine time.

# Some Final Thoughts

Never forget that your goal is consistency, not quantity. It may seem overwhelming and a long way off to think about adding entire chapters to your routine time. But if you are consistent and confident, not putting yourself under pressure, and yet exercising daily discipline, you will be surprised how much you will have memorized in a month, and amazed at what you have memorized in a year.

Take the challenge, and be an example. Honor God's Word by hiding it in your heart and meditating on it day and night. God says that you will be like a tree planted by the rivers of water and whatever you do shall prosper. May God bless you and strengthen you for the task.

# About the Author

Dr. Morris graduated from Pacific Coast Baptist Bible College and Anchor Theological Seminary. He received his Ph.D. in Biblical Studies from Louisiana Baptist University. Since 1978, he and his wife, Debbie, have served as missionaries in Chiapas, Mexico. He presently pastors the Baptist church he founded in Tuxtla Gutiérrez and oversees several other churches, missions and a Christian school. Much of his time is dedicated to training Hispanic pastors, and counseling.

To learn more about Dr. Morris and his wife Debbie, pray for them, or to support them, please do so by using the links on the next page.

Visit www.dandebbiemorris.com

Visit www.ibbh.org, their Mexico church website

If you benefited from this book, please post a review on Amazon or tell others about it on Facebook.